Three Plays

Copyright © Nick Voro 2025

All rights reserved. No part of this publication may be reproduced or transmitted in any form or by any means, electronic or mechanical, including photocopying, recording, or any information storage and retrieval system, without permission in writing from the publisher.

First Edition

Three Plays

VoroBooks, Etobicoke, Ontario, Canada

ISBN: 978-1-7383199-9-2

Typesetting and additional design by Lee Thompson Editing+

To contact the author: Nick_Voro@hotmail.com

This is a work of fiction. Names, characters, places and incidents either are products of the author's imagination or are used fictitiously. Any resemblance to actual events or locales or persons, living or dead, is entirely coincidental.

MY HAUNTED LIFE

My Haunted Life

THE CHARACTERS

MAN – A man in his 40s.
WOMAN – A woman in her 40s.

THE SCENE

A moving car.

My Haunted Life

MAN: What do you see when you close your eyes?

WOMAN: Nothing. (*Pause.*) What about you?

MAN: I can't close my eyes. I'm driving.

WOMAN: Just for a second…

MAN: I see you.

WOMAN: That's because you were just looking at me.

MAN: No, I wasn't. I was looking at the road. (*Pause.*) I wish every time I closed my eyes… I could see you without other imagery intruding. To close my eyes, and for only you to be there. Every single time.

WOMAN: Now now. Don't be greedy. Not

Conversational Therapy

seeing me every time, all the time, gives you a chance to miss me. And then when we finally see each other it's...

MAN: Ignited gunpowder.

WOMAN: Fireworks.

MAN: You know, when we first met, I would watch you sleep for hours on end. I'd hardly blink, just stare at your rising and falling chest.

WOMAN: Why were you afraid to blink?

MAN: I was afraid that if I closed my eyes, by the time I opened them again, you would be gone.

WOMAN: Not the type to usually vanish without saying goodbye.

MAN: I couldn't imagine my life without you.

WOMAN: Try. What would you do?

MAN: I think I would live among my memories of you, opt for make-believe. Nostalgia, lost in the immediacy of the transpired moment.

My Haunted Life

A permanent resident in a fantasy world I've created.

WOMAN: Sounds like the perfect opportunity to reflect on your life. Your past, present, perhaps even future.

MAN: There could never be thoughts about the future without you around. I would be like a patient on life support suddenly unplugged, just those seven minutes of reminiscences about you, and then I would fade away.

WOMAN: If you had to pick only one memory, which one would it be?

MAN: You aren't making it easy, are you?

WOMAN: Where would the fun be in that?

MAN: It'd have to be your last birthday. When we splurged on a weekend we really couldn't afford to stay at that fancy hotel spa place.

WOMAN: Great sex, but even better food.

(*He throws his hands up in protest of culinary*

wonders beating out sexual escapades.)

But why that day? What made it so special to you?

MAN: Just the fact that I have never seen you so relaxed. You were calm and vulnerable. You really opened up to me.

WOMAN: And that's when you felt comfortable enough to tell me you loved me.

MAN: The setting was perfect and the moment too precious to waste. It's been on my mind for a while. I felt a great relief and a great warmth when I uttered those words for the very first time.

WOMAN: And you haven't stopped saying them since.

MAN: I never want to stop saying them. I love saying them.

WOMAN: And what about the worst memory? The one that haunts you the most.

MAN: Should I even have one of those?

WOMAN: Stop being cheeky. Every couple has one of those. And it's probably the one you replay the most in your mind.

MAN: Even over the best one?

WOMAN: We always tend to remember the negative memories more. Don't ask me why, I am not a psychologist, but there's something about them; they stick out and get stuck in our memory banks.

MAN: (*He frowns.*) Well, there is one…

WOMAN: I knew there was. You just don't like to talk about it.

MAN: I don't. It hurts too much to say it out loud.

WOMAN: Well, now is your chance to tell me.

MAN: Do you remember when we both developed that obsession, that preoccupation with the paranormal?

Conversational Therapy

WOMAN: Yes. We can thank reality television for that.

MAN: Right. And we decided to take a road trip to Bodie.

WOMAN: Bodie…

MAN: Remember that abandoned mining town.

WOMAN: I do. Yes. I remember now. Strange, I had forgotten about that.

MAN: I wish I could.

WOMAN: Keep going, help me with my recollection.

MAN: We got there and…

WOMAN: It turned out to be exactly as advertised. Not a soul around.

MAN: If you keep interrupting, I won't bother to tell it at all.

WOMAN: Go ahead. I will be the definition of quietude.

My Haunted Life

MAN: We got there. And it was abandoned, just like you said. But that wasn't it. There was something else. Something I hadn't counted on. The silence of the place. How sharp it was. Crawling under your skin. A silence with a set of eyes, never letting you get out of its sight. Just us surrounded by this silence and the deathly stillness. I told you to wait in the car while I looked around.

WOMAN: I didn't listen.

MAN: Of course, you didn't. You are too fiercely independent for something like that.

WOMAN: I got scared of being alone in the car. I also didn't want you out there by yourself.

MAN: Whatever happened to staying quiet and listening?

WOMAN: Too fiercely independent, remember? A real problem when it comes to compliance.

MAN: (*Sighs.*) I remember. (*Pause.*) So we both left the car and went to explore. We ended up at this building. It was larger than all the rest. My mind raced standing next to it, and for a split second I actually thought it might be the source of all this enshrouding silence. It, I swear it seemed to call out to me, *Open the door and step inside.*

WOMAN: Right! And then we heard a noise...

MAN: I turned around to see what it was, but I couldn't see anything. The sun was setting, darkness encroaching. And when I turned back to tell you not to worry, you weren't there. Only your footsteps remained imprinted on the soft ground. A trail I was able to follow right to the front door of the mysterious building. The door was slightly ajar. I called out to you, but you never responded. I rushed inside, but I couldn't find you anywhere. There were no footprints inside the building. Where did you go? (*Pause.*) What did you do there? (*Pause.*) Why won't you answer me?

PSYCHIATRIST'S PSYCHIATRIST

Psychiatrist's Psychiatrist

THE CHARACTERS

DR. DAVID MURPHY – A man in his 20s.
DISTRESSED WOMAN – A woman of 30.

THE SCENE

A psychiatrist's office.

Psychiatrist's Psychiatrist

A sparsely decorated room with a well-used couch, some paintings and a few diplomas hung on the walls, a single window with a view of the cityscape/concrete jungle and a desk behind which sits the psychiatrist, DR. DAVID MURPHY.

His youthfulness sticks out like a sore thumb. Sitting at his desk, he is absentmindedly reading some papers when he is interrupted by the slightly older DISTRESSED WOMAN who barges inside his office unannounced and without a proper appointment.

DR. DAVID MURPHY: (*Sits up. Startled.*) Can I help you?

DISTRESSED WOMAN: Well, that's what I am here to find out.

DR. DAVID MURPHY: I am glad you came

Conversational Therapy

to me for help. But please keep in mind for any future sessions, two of my biggest pet peeves happen to be self-assurance and individuals barging in without properly scheduled appointments. What if I was with a patient?

DISTRESSED WOMAN: It doesn't seem like you get too many clients.

DR. DAVID MURPHY: What makes you say that?

DISTRESSED WOMAN: (*She looks around the office.*) Well... there's no receptionist. You are the only person here. (*Pause.*) And why don't you like self-assurance? It's an admirable quality. Barging in I can understand, although I was raised in a family that considers showing up on time better left to the low earning wage dependant working class who can't stand to lose a minute.

DR. DAVID MURPHY: I am used to women lacking assertiveness, distressed women on the brink of suicide who have a hard time finding my office. (*Pause.*) And preferably well-mannered ones that knock before they enter.

DISTRESSED WOMAN: (*Shrugs.*) Oh well, I can assure you that I am very suicidal. (*She begins to pace the office, pausing to look at the diplomas and the cheap paintings.*) I just want to make sure you are the right fit for me before I fall apart on your comfy couch.

DR. DAVID MURPHY: Was the last psychiatrist the wrong fit?

DISTRESSED WOMAN, *mysteriously*: Well, you could say that.

DR. DAVID MURPHY: Is that what YOU would say?

DISTRESSED WOMAN: (*She approaches the window; it is dirty and smudged. Her hands grip the bottom, and with great effort she gets it to slide up. She leans halfway out and looks down.*) I would say he was the WRONG FIT. I mean, what else can one say about a man who jumps out of a twelfth-story window, shatters all over the sidewalk below and leaves behind a big puddle of blood.

DR. DAVID MURPHY: That sounds horrific.

DISTRESSED WOMAN, *wickedly*: No, the horrific part was the blood geyser that splashed innocent children and their cones next to an ice cream truck. (*Pause.*) That might stay with them for a while.

DR. DAVID MURPHY, *confused*: You have an interesting sense of humor.

DISTRESSED WOMAN: All morbid people have that.

DR. DAVID MURPHY: Maybe you should try your hand at stand-up comedy.

DISTRESSED WOMAN: I would rather not drive people to commit suicide.

DR. DAVID MURPHY: You just want to commit it yourself.

DISTRESSED WOMAN, *thoughtfully*: Maybe and maybe not. What I didn't want was to remain

Psychiatrist's Psychiatrist

stagnant and do absolutely nothing. Just me, myself and I locked away in a glass cage waiting for a rock to shatter my existence.

DR. DAVID MURPHY: So, you reached out for help.

DISTRESSED WOMAN: Or so I thought I did. Until... (*Pause.*)

DR. DAVID MURPHY: Your therapist jumped. (*Pause.*) It must have come as such a shock to receive that call.

DISTRESSED WOMAN: Oh, there was no call. He jumped in front of me.

DR. DAVID MURPHY: You mean...?

DISTRESSED WOMAN: Yes, we were having a session.

DR. DAVID MURPHY: And what did he say?

DISTRESSED WOMAN: "I need to get some fresh air." He walked to the window, opened

Conversational Therapy

it, and climbed out.

DR. DAVID MURPHY, *incredulously*: Did he look back at you?

DISTRESSED WOMAN: Yes, he did. He was smiling.

DR. DAVID MURPHY: He smiled?

DISTRESSED WOMAN: Smiled and then winked.

DR. DAVID MURPHY: He winked at you? You sure it was not just something in his eye?

DISTRESSED WOMAN: No, he definitely winked at me.

DR. DAVID MURPHY: I wonder what it meant.

DISTRESSED WOMAN: I don't think there's any subtext to it. He just winked. I mean, the whole thing was sort of funny.

DR. DAVID MURPHY: (*Shakes his head.*) He must have been stressed out with his practice and

Psychiatrist's Psychiatrist

patients and literally gone to pieces over his work.

DISTRESSED WOMAN: His body was remarkably whole, albeit a bit pancake-like. (*Pause.*) And I highly doubt it was his work considering I was his only patient.

DR. DAVID MURPHY: His only patient?

DISTRESSED WOMAN: Well, after he took up my case and we started to sleep together, he dropped everyone else. He told me no one mattered except me.

DR. DAVID MURPHY: You were sleeping with him?

DISTRESSED WOMAN: Is that so uncommon? I almost always thought of it as a job perk in this profession.

DR. DAVID MURPHY: I can reassure you that not all of us sleep with our patients.

DISTRESSED WOMAN, *smilingly*: If you actually had patients. I am sure you would want to.

Conversational Therapy

DR. DAVID MURPHY, *helplessly*: I... (*Pause.*)

DISTRESSED WOMAN: Come on, Doc, can you imagine sniveling, vulnerable women with low-cut dresses laying on your couch all day long telling you their innermost secrets, putting you in a position of power over them. You are telling me that wouldn't get your dick hard?

DR. DAVID MURPHY: (*Nervously coughs.*) My penis should not be of any concern to you at this moment.

DISTRESSED WOMAN: Well, Doc, for now, you can keep it to yourself. I am sure eventually it will pop out during one of our future sessions. They always do. (*She winks at him.*) I like you. You can consider me your first official patient. Just don't jump on me. Remember, I'm the one with the issues. (*She walks out of the office.*)

CLASS DISTINCTIONS

Class Distinctions

THE CHARACTERS

YOUNG WOMAN – A woman in her 20s.
HOMELESS YOUTH – A man in his 20s.

THE SCENE

A subway station.

Class Distinctions

A busy subway station. People rushing to their destinations at a maddening pace with no regard for anyone else's personal space.

HOMELESS YOUTH, 20-something, disheveled and hungry, is sitting on the floor of the station watching this human traffic pass him by. There is a hat with a few coins next to his feet.

YOUNG WOMAN, urbanite, eloquent in her movements but with an intense gaze, catches his eye when she tries to walk past without acknowledging him.

    HOMELESS YOUTH, *challengingly*: You don't have a heart.

    YOUNG WOMAN: (*She stops, taken aback by*

his direct approach.) Excuse me?

HOMELESS YOUTH, *persistently*: I said... you don't have a heart.

YOUNG WOMAN: If I didn't have a beating heart, I wouldn't be alive right now, standing here talking to you.

HOMELESS YOUTH, *cockily*: That's not the kind of heart I was talking about.

YOUNG WOMAN: So not the physical but the spiritual type, right? The kind that's capable of things like compassion, sympathy and empathy.

HOMELESS YOUTH: That's exactly the type I was talking about. (*Pause.*) So knowing all this, why do you pass me every day, Monday to Friday, and have never once found it in yourself to spare me some change? (*Pause.*) All you do is give me that long glance as you walk past. That's why I said you don't have a heart.

YOUNG WOMAN: Because I acknowledge

Class Distinctions

you but don't find myself reaching into my purse for money that I slave for every single day to just hand over to you for what... just sitting there?

HOMELESS YOUTH: That's exactly right.

YOUNG WOMAN: (*She laughs from sheer disbelief.*) You have some nerve. Do you ever stop and think about anyone but yourself? The world doesn't revolve around you just because you are sitting on the floor of a subway station begging for change in the financial district of the city.

HOMELESS YOUTH: And what about you? Strutting around like you're on a catwalk. This isn't a fashion show. You walk around like you own it all.

YOUNG WOMAN: Own what? The subway platform? I think the city owns that.

HOMELESS YOUTH: A wisecracking privileged girl wearing a designer coat...

(*She interrupts him.*)

YOUNG WOMAN: You still haven't told me

Conversational Therapy

what I own. What exactly is that in your opinion? Please clue me in about my supposed riches.

HOMELESS YOUTH: You own this. (*He gesticulates all around him.*) All this! (*Pause.*) Entitlement is a disease that infects many. You are clearly a victim of it.

YOUNG WOMAN: And you are clearly a victim of bad choices and poverty. But that's obvious. What isn't so obvious is why you're channelling a terrible car salesman, trying so desperately hard to sell me something without paying an iota of attention to my needs as a customer... which in this case is to leave the showroom and get on with my day.

HOMELESS YOUTH: What is it that I am trying to sell you exactly?

YOUNG WOMAN: You are selling an idea. You prey on strong, successful women, and then you attack them for being strong and having money. You pick away at their confidence to bring

Class Distinctions

them down a few notches, just so you can make them feel guilty for being where they are. For having what they have. You are selling the idea of *YOU*.

HOMELESS YOUTH: People around here have money to spare. They sure make enough of it.

YOUNG WOMAN: And you want some of it. But just because someone dresses nicely or walks a certain way doesn't necessarily mean they have money. Some do, and some don't. People from all walks of life and social classes are willing to contribute. Some more readily than others. The ones that aren't so quick to give had probably asked themselves a very good question: What will the money purchase? (*Pause.*) So, what will you purchase with that money?

HOMELESS YOUTH: (*He grimaces. His face deformed by anger.*) That's none of your business!

YOUNG WOMAN: (*She smiles broadly.*) It's

my money. That makes it my business.

HOMELESS YOUTH: Not once you have handed it over.

YOUNG WOMAN: But have I handed it over? I haven't, have I? (*Pause.*) I want you to broaden your horizons, expand your mind beyond the beggar's mentality, past the one-way transaction of a perfectly capable individual who shuns employment to freeload. Start looking at it from a business perspective. It's a donation that comes with a price.

HOMELESS YOUTH: (*He spits on the ground over his left shoulder.*) Good old upper classes and their fucked-up legislature. So, tell me, what's the price?

YOUNG WOMAN: An assurance that you won't senselessly spend the money. Convince me. Clarify the end destination. Intended purpose for my contribution. If I had to guess, a liquor store. Or drugs that you'd administer hopefully at a

Class Distinctions

safe injection site. Cigarettes, booze, and drugs. The nourishment of the destitute and the broken. (*Pause.*) So, are you going to tell me? Or do I just go on guessing? It's the only way to get me to reach inside my purse and give you something.

HOMELESS YOUTH, *defensively*: I don't have to do anything.

YOUNG WOMAN: I can see that. Why would you? You have retired; you yearn for nothing having acquired all those worldly possessions you coveted in your earlier years, through your perseverance and hard work you are now living comfortably in a spacious outmoded house. Of course, you no longer have to do anything. (*She smiles ruthlessly.*) Now if you can accompany me back to reality for a moment. I get it, maybe you haven't taken any business courses, but this is a business transaction like any other. Wouldn't you agree?

HOMELESS YOUTH: No, I would not.

Conversational Therapy

YOUNG WOMAN: Really? Because it seems to me that we both want something from one another. Look, I know you can't afford a financial consultant, so let me give you some advice, free of charge. People like knowing where their money is going, which is what your beggar's sign seems to be lacking. I have a marker on me. If you want, we can add that in right now. Of course, you'd have to tell me what it is that you are going to do with this cash, which brings us right back to where we started.

HOMELESS YOUTH: (*He laughs.*) Cash... people barely spare change. You're telling me if I tell you what I will use this money for, you'll give me more than just change.

YOUNG WOMAN: You'd be surprised what people are willing do for others if they truly believe in their intentions.

HOMELESS YOUTH: You haven't answered my question.

Class Distinctions

YOUNG WOMAN: It would have to be something I believe in.

HOMELESS YOUTH: So, there's a catch.

YOUNG WOMAN: Everything in life comes with a catch. There's no such thing as free money.

HOMELESS YOUTH: What about the people who give me whatever change they have and walk away without even waiting for a thank you?

YOUNG WOMAN: A guilty conscience can be a strong persuader.

HOMELESS YOUTH: Which is something you don't seem to suffer from.

YOUNG WOMAN: You are right; I don't. I didn't get to where I am by walking over corpse-strewn sidewalks; my conscience is untroubled. When I donate, I donate out of the goodness of my heart, not because of some terrible pangs of guilt. I donate because I care, not because I am trying to purchase a first-class ticket to heaven through carefully calculated financial contributions.

Conversational Therapy

HOMELESS YOUTH: No, you clearly got there by being a frigid, greedy, and all-around judgmental bitch.

YOUNG WOMAN: Well, that's why I am wearing Christian Louboutin leather pumps and you... have bags wrapped around your feet. That's a pretty clear distinction if I ever seen one painted so vividly. So, are you going to tell me about your intentions, or should I go?

HOMELESS YOUTH, *barely audible*: Fucking bitch.

YOUNG WOMAN: What was that?!

HOMELESS YOUTH: Nothing... so you want to know about my intentions.

YOUNG WOMAN: Yes, dying to hear about those.

HOMELESS YOUTH: I would use the money to get some food to help me concentrate as I flip through the classifieds looking for a job.

YOUNG WOMAN: Funny... the scars on

Class Distinctions

your arm tell a different story. People lie, track marks unerringly record the truth. You can't refute an accurately kept record jotted down one prick at a time.

(*The Homeless Youth rolls down his sleeves.*)

YOUNG WOMAN: A piece of advice. Switch to a cheaper drug of choice. Try crack. More affordable and you might even have some leftover change to buy yourself some food.

HOMELESS YOUTH: What is your fucking problem?!

YOUNG WOMAN: I don't have a problem. You seem to be the one with the problem. My wallet is actually quite full. You are the one with lint in his pockets. I am just trying to help you out with some sound advice.

HOMELESS YOUTH: I don't want your sound advice; I want your fucking money, lady.

YOUNG WOMAN: I know you do. But if you want my money, you must earn it. And being a demanding junkie is not the best way to go about it. Anyone ever teach you manners when you were younger?

HOMELESS YOUTH: What do you know about my upbringing?

YOUNG WOMAN: I never said I did but spare me what comes next. I don't want to hear your sappy story about not having parents and being stuck in a foster home, and this is exactly why you ended up here today. I don't care. What I care about is what you are doing now, today, tomorrow, about getting off these streets.

HOMELESS YOUTH: And what about you, miss perfect? What's your drug of choice? A glass of wine every night before bed? Maybe the whole bottle?

YOUNG WOMAN: I don't drink.

HOMELESS YOUTH: Everyone drinks.

YOUNG WOMAN: I don't. My parents were alcoholics.

Class Distinctions

HOMELESS YOUTH: At least you had parents.

YOUNG WOMAN: What did I tell you about sappy stories from your past? I don't care. You look hurt. I have some tissues in my purse next to my wallet if you want to wipe away those tears in your eyes.

HOMELESS YOUTH: Fuck You!

YOUNG WOMAN: I don't usually fuck unemployed men. I do have some standards. Hey, I have an idea. Let's try to find you a job and then you can maybe ask me out. No guarantees I will say yes.

HOMELESS YOUTH: Do you know how many people die out here every day because of heartless people like you?

YOUNG WOMAN: I don't think anyone dies in the actual station. They die out there. In the streets.

HOMELESS YOUTH: What difference does that make!

Conversational Therapy

YOUNG WOMAN: I don't know. I've just always been a stickler for details, which is why you currently aren't in possession of my money.

HOMELESS YOUTH: Fuck you!

YOUNG WOMAN: We have already been over this. The answer is still no. Cheer up! You are young. You aren't suffering from schizophrenia, and life expectancy for a homeless person is around thirty-nine years. Still a long time to go before you die. It's a gradual process. Don't sweat it, bud. You will live to see tomorrow and put in another solid appearance at your job as a professional panhandler.

HOMELESS YOUTH, *angrily*: I seriously want to kick your teeth in.

YOUNG WOMAN: Violence is never the answer. But since you seem to be having such a tough time with donations toward your very charitable cause, I would suggest you pack up for the day and go to a shelter. A warm bed and a

Class Distinctions

meal usually beat a cold marble floor.

HOMELESS YOUTH: Do you know what it costs to keep a youth in a shelter? Thirty to forty grand a year.

YOUNG WOMAN: That sounds about right. What's your point? Where are you heading with this?

HOMELESS YOUTH: Lack of available spots. That's where I was heading with this.

YOUNG WOMAN: I am going to call your bluff and pull your card. Are you seriously trying to tell me that every single shelter in this city is at full capacity? If one is full, you try another one.

HOMELESS YOUTH: And how do you expect me to know whether they are full or not?

YOUNG WOMAN: Ever heard of that nifty Alexander Graham Bell invention called the telephone? There's a payphone right outside this station; all you need is some change... (*She looks down at his hat on the ground.*) ...which I see you already have.

HOMELESS YOUTH: What made you such a cold analytical realist?

YOUNG WOMAN: Life in general. Also living on the streets, begging for money, and sleeping in shelters. You don't remember me, Sam, but we used to sit on corners side by side cuddling together for body heat. Just us against the savage elements of an indifferent society.

HOMELESS YOUTH: (*He slowly processes the information, slack-jawed, shocked.*) Chrissy?

YOUNG WOMAN: I see your memory is still intact. It just needed some prodding.

HOMELESS YOUTH: How did you...

YOUNG WOMAN: I got help, Sam. Shelters can be amazing at connecting you with the right people. All you have to want is something more than a handout. (*She reaches in her purse and offers him a card.*

Class Distinctions

CHRISTINE BIRDWELL.
SHELTER DEPUTY MANAGER.)

ABOUT THE AUTHOR

A native of Kyiv, Ukraine, but living in Canada since the age of eleven, Nick Voro discovered literature at an early age, never quite mustering the ability to put an excellent book down. A recent graduate of the Toronto Film School, Nick divides his time between being a full-time parent and a full-time author.

His debut work, *Conversational Therapy: Stories and Plays*, has recently sold over 200 copies and is part of the library system (United States, Canada, New Zealand, Australia and Scotland).

Lee D. Thompson, an editor and writer from Moncton, New Brunswick, Canada, edited this short story. His books include: a novel in [xxx] dreams from Broken Jaw Press, Mouth Human Must Die from Frog Hollow Press and Apastoral: A Mistopia from Corona/Samizdat. His short fiction has been published in many anthologies, including Random House's Victory Meat, New Fiction from Atlantic Canada and Vagrant Press's The Vagrant Revue of New Fiction. He is the winner of the David Adams Richards Prize (2018) and New Brunswick Book Award (2022). He is the publisher of Galleon Books.

www.ingramcontent.com/pod-product-compliance
Lightning Source LLC
Chambersburg PA
CBHW071917070526
44583CB00016B/2031